REVOLUTIONIZE YOUR BUSINESS

Proven Strategies for Transforming Your Company and Driving Success

HIVE D. SPARK

This book is intended to provide general information relating to business improvement and strategies. It is not intended to be a comprehensive guide and should not be used as a substitute for professional advice.

TABLE OF CONTENT

INTRODUCTION

BUSINESS IMPROVEMENT

As the owner of a small business, I was always looking for ways to improve and grow my company. However, I found that I often hit a roadblock when it came to implementing new ideas and making meaningful changes.

One day, I decided to seek out some outside help and hired a business consultant to assess the current state of my business and provide recommendations for improvement. After conducting a thorough analysis, the consultant presented me with a report detailing several areas of my business that could be improved upon.

One of the main areas of focus was my marketing strategy. My business was heavily reliant on word-of-mouth referrals and I had not invested much in paid advertising or social media marketing. The consultant showed me the potential for reaching a wider audience and attracting new customers through targeted online marketing efforts.

I was initially hesitant to invest in these types of marketing efforts, as I was unsure of the return on investment. However, the consultant assured me that with a well-planned and executed strategy, the results would be worth it.

I decided to take the plunge and invest in a comprehensive online marketing campaign. The results were impressive. My website traffic increased significantly and I saw a noticeable uptick in new customers. Additionally, my overall brand visibility improved as more people became aware of my business.

The success of this campaign convinced me of the importance of continuous business improvement. I learned that by staying open to new ideas and being willing to make necessary changes, I was able to significantly improve my business and achieve greater success.

Since then, I have continued to seek out opportunities for growth and improvement, and my business has continued to thrive as a result. I highly recommend that all business owners take a proactive approach to improve their operations and be open to seeking outside help when necessary. The benefits of business improvement are immeasurable and can lead to long-term success and stability

CHAPTER ONE

IDENTIFYING AREAS OF IMPROVEMENT

Business improvement refers to the process of identifying and implementing changes to a company or organization to increase efficiency, productivity, and overall performance. It involves analyzing current business processes and identifying areas for improvement, as well as implementing strategies and solutions to address these areas. Business improvement can involve a wide range of activities, including process optimization, quality control, cost reduction, and customer satisfaction.

Effective business improvement requires a systematic approach and the ability to identify and prioritize opportunities for improvement. It also requires the ability to gather and analyze data, as well as to develop and implement solutions that address identified issues. By continuously seeking ways to improve, businesses can stay competitive and achieve long-term success.

Identifying areas of improvement in a business is a crucial step toward its growth and success. It helps to identify areas where the business is falling short and takes corrective measures to improve its performance. Here are some steps to identify areas of improvement in a business:

Analyze your business data: Data analysis is a key tool to identify areas of improvement in a business. By analyzing data such as sales, customer feedback, and employee performance, you can identify patterns and trends that highlight areas where the business is performing well and areas that need improvement.

Conduct a SWOT analysis: A SWOT analysis is a useful tool to identify the strengths, weaknesses, opportunities, and threats of a business. It helps to identify areas of improvement by highlighting the business's weaknesses and threats, which can be addressed through targeted strategies and actions.

Seek feedback from customers: Customers are a valuable source of feedback on a business's performance. By soliciting feedback through surveys, focus groups, or online reviews, businesses can gather insights on areas where they are falling short and where they can improve.

Engage with employees: Employees are on the front lines of a business and often have valuable insights on areas that need improvement. By engaging with employees through regular meetings, surveys, or focus groups, businesses can gather valuable feedback and ideas for improvement.

Monitor industry trends: Keeping track of industry trends can help a business identify areas where it is lagging and needs to improve. By staying up-to-date on the latest trends and developments, businesses can stay ahead of the curve and make necessary changes to remain competitive.

Implementing changes based on these areas of improvement can help a business grow and succeed. It is important to regularly review and assess the effectiveness of these changes to ensure that the business is making progress toward its goals

Assessing Internal Processes

Internal processes are the series of activities that a business undertakes to produce goods or services. These processes can range from simple tasks such as answering customer inquiries to complex operations like manufacturing a product. Assessing these internal processes is an important step in any business improvement plan, as it allows a company to identify inefficiencies and make changes to increase efficiency and effectiveness.

There are several steps involved in assessing internal processes for business improvement such as:

1. **Identify the process:** Determine which internal processes need to be assessed. This could include any process that is critical to the success of the business, such as manufacturing, sales, or customer service.

2. **Define the process:** Clearly define the steps involved in each process and document them in a flowchart or process map. This will help to identify any bottlenecks or inefficiencies in the process.

3. **Gather data:** Collect data on the process, such as time spent on each step, number of errors, and customer feedback. Using this information, the areas that need improvement may be identified.

4. **Analyze the data:** Use the data collected to identify trends and patterns. Look for opportunities to streamline the process, eliminate unnecessary steps, or automate tasks.

5. **Implement improvements:** Based on the analysis, implement changes to the process to improve efficiency and effectiveness. This could include introducing new technology, revising procedures, or reallocating resources.

6. **Monitor and evaluate:** Monitor the process to ensure that the improvements are having the desired effect and make any necessary adjustments.

Assessing internal processes is an ongoing process, as business needs and priorities are constantly evolving. By regularly reviewing and improving internal processes, businesses can ensure that they are operating at peak efficiency and meeting the needs of their customers.

Examining Customer Service

Here are a few ways to examine customer service in business improvement:

1. **Conduct customer surveys:** Surveys are a great way to gather direct feedback from your customers about their experiences with your customer service. You may then make the necessary modifications after identifying any areas that require improvement.

2. **Monitor social media:** Social media can be a great source of

information about customer experiences with your business. Keep an eye on what people are saying about your customer service on platforms like Twitter, Facebook, and Instagram.

3. **Analyze customer service metrics:** There are several metrics you can track to get a sense of how well your customer service is performing. These might include things like average response time, resolution rate, and customer satisfaction scores.

4. **Observe customer interactions:** Observing customer interactions can provide valuable insights into how

well your customer service team is performing. You can do this by listening in on phone calls, watching in-person interactions, or reviewing recorded interactions.

5. **Train and empower your customer service team:** Make sure your customer service team has the skills and resources they need to effectively serve your customers. This might involve providing training, setting clear expectations, and giving them the autonomy to make decisions that will benefit the customer

CHAPTER TWO

ANALYZING FINANCIAL PERFORMANCE

Analyzing financial performance is an essential aspect of business improvement and growth. By examining various financial metrics and ratios, businesses can gain valuable insights into the health and efficiency of their operations. This can help inform strategic decision-making and allow for targeted improvements to be made to drive profitability and competitiveness.

Many different financial performance metrics can be analyzed, including:

1. **Revenue:** This is the total amount of money that a business generates from the sale of its goods or services. Analyzing revenue trends over time can help a business understand the demand for its products and identify growth opportunities.

2. **Gross margin:** This is the difference between a business's revenue and the cost of goods sold. A high gross margin indicates that a business can generate a significant amount of profit from each sale.

3. **Operating margin:** This is the difference between a business's revenue and its operating expenses. A high operating margin indicates that a

business can generate a significant amount of profit after covering its overhead costs.

4. **Net income:** This is the profit that a business generates after accounting for all of its revenues and expenses. This is often considered the bottom line of a business and is an important measure of its overall financial performance.

5. **Return on investment (ROI)**: This is a measure of the profitability of an investment. It is calculated by dividing the net income generated by the investment by the initial cost of the investment. A high ROI indicates that an investment is generating a

significant amount of profit relative to its cost.

6. **Liquidity ratios:** These ratios measure a business's ability to meet its short-term financial obligations. Examples include the current ratio, which measures a business's ability to pay off its current liabilities with its current assets, and the quick ratio, which measures a business's ability to pay off its current liabilities with its most liquid assets.

By analyzing these and other financial performance metrics, businesses can identify areas of strength and weakness, and develop strategies for improvement. For example, if a business has a low gross margin, it may need to focus on reducing the cost of goods sold to increase profitability. Alternatively, if a business has a high operating margin but a low net income, it may need to focus on reducing its non-operating expenses to boost profitability.

Overall, analyzing financial performance is a critical aspect of business improvement and growth. By examining various financial metrics and ratios, businesses can gain valuable insights into the efficiency and profitability of their operations, and develop strategies for improvement.

Setting Goals for Improvement

Setting goals is a crucial step in the process of improving a business. By setting clear and specific goals, you can focus your efforts and resources on the areas that will have the greatest impact on your business. It can also help to keep you motivated and accountable as you work towards achieving your objectives. Here are some tips for setting goals for the improvement of your business:

1. **Start with a vision:** Before you can set goals, it's important to have a clear idea of what you want to achieve. This could be a long-term vision for the direction of your business or a more specific objective related to a specific area of your business.

2. **Make your goals SMART:** To make your goals more effective, make sure they are Specific, Measurable, Attainable, Relevant, and Time-bound. This will help you to create clear and achievable objectives that you can work towards.

3. **Involve your team:** Engage your team in the goal-setting process. By involving them in the process, you can tap into their expertise and ideas and create a sense of ownership and commitment to achieving the goals.

4. **Set priorities:** With limited time and resources, it's important to prioritize your goals. Consider the potential

impact of each goal and the resources required to achieve it. This will help you to focus on the most important goals and allocate your resources effectively.

5. **Monitor progress:** Regularly track your progress toward your goals and make adjustments as needed. This will help you to stay on track and make sure you are making progress towards your objectives.

By setting clear and specific goals, you can focus your efforts and resources on the areas that will have the greatest impact, and track your progress along the way.

Developing an improvement plan

Developing an Improvement Plan in a business is an essential step toward achieving long-term success and growth. It allows a company to identify areas for improvement, set goals, and create a roadmap for achieving those goals. By regularly reviewing and updating the Improvement Plan, a business can adapt to changing market conditions and customer needs, and continually strive for excellence.

Here are some key points to consider when developing an Improvement Plan:

- **Identify areas for improvement:** The first step in creating an Improvement Plan is to identify areas of the business that could benefit from improvement. This could include processes, products, services, customer satisfaction, efficiency, or any other aspect of the business.

- **Set clear goals:** Once you have identified areas for improvement, it's important to set clear, specific, and measurable goals for each area. This will help to ensure that progress is being made toward achieving the desired improvements.

- **Develop a roadmap**: Once you have set your goals, it's important to create a roadmap for achieving them. This should include specific steps and tasks that need to be completed, as well as timelines and resources required.

- **Involve employees:** Engaging employees in the Improvement Plan process can be extremely valuable. Not only will they have valuable insights and ideas for improvement, but they will also be more invested in the success of the plan if they have a say in its development.

- **Review and update regularly:** It's important to regularly review and update the Improvement Plan to ensure that it is still relevant and aligned with the needs of the business. This can be done regularly, such as annually or quarterly, to ensure that the business is continuously improving and adapting to changing market conditions.

Implementing an Improvement Plan can be a challenging but rewarding process. By following these steps and involving key stakeholders, a business can make meaningful progress toward achieving its goals and becoming more successful

CHAPTER THREE

EVALUATING PERFORMANCE

Evaluating performance in business improvement is an essential aspect of running a successful organization. It helps to identify areas of the business that are working well and those that need improvement, as well as to track progress over time.

There are several key steps involved in evaluating performance in business improvement:

1. **Set clear goals and objectives:** Before you can evaluate performance,

you need to have a clear understanding of what you are trying to achieve. This includes setting specific, measurable, achievable, relevant, and time-bound (SMART) goals and objectives.

2. **Identify the key performance indicators (KPIs):** Once you have set your goals and objectives, you need to determine how you will measure progress toward achieving them. This involves identifying the key performance indicators (KPIs) that will provide insight into the performance of your business. These may include financial metrics such as revenue and profit, as well as non-financial metrics such as

customer satisfaction and employee engagement.

3. **Collect and analyze data:** To accurately evaluate performance, you need to collect and analyze data on your KPIs. This may involve using tools such as dashboards, spreadsheets, or software to track and analyze your data.

4. **Communicate results:** It's important to share the results of your performance evaluation with the appropriate stakeholders, including employees, managers, and board members. This can help to identify areas of strength and weakness and

provide guidance for future improvement efforts.

5. **Take action:** Based on the results of your performance evaluation, you should take action to address any areas of weakness and continue to build on areas of strength. This may involve implementing new processes, adjusting resources, or making changes to your business model.

By regularly setting goals, tracking progress, and taking action to address areas of weakness, you can continuously improve your business and achieve long-term success.

Strategic Planning

Strategic planning is an essential process for any business looking to improve and grow. It involves setting long-term goals and objectives, analyzing the internal and external environment in which the business operates, and developing plans and strategies to achieve those goals.

One key aspect of strategic planning is the SWOT analysis, which stands for Strengths, Weaknesses, Opportunities, and Threats. This analysis helps a business identify its internal strengths and weaknesses, as well as external opportunities and threats. By understanding these factors, a business can develop strategies to leverage its strengths and opportunities while addressing its weaknesses and threats.

Another important aspect of strategic planning is stakeholder analysis, which involves identifying and analyzing the needs and expectations of all parties that have an interest in or impact on the business. This includes customers, employees, shareholders, suppliers, and the local community, among others. By understanding the needs and expectations of these stakeholders, a business can develop strategies that align with its interests and goals.

Once a business has completed its SWOT analysis and stakeholder analysis, it can begin to develop specific strategies and action plans to achieve its long-term goals. This may involve identifying new markets to enter, developing new products or services, implementing cost-cutting measures, or improving internal processes and systems.

Effective strategic planning requires strong leadership and collaboration among team members, as well as regular review and revision to ensure that the business is on track to achieve its goals. By following a structured and thorough strategic planning process, businesses can improve their operations and position themselves for long-term success

Strategic Analysis

Strategic analysis is a crucial step in the business improvement process. It involves evaluating an organization's current situation, analyzing its internal and external environments, and identifying opportunities for growth and success.

Several tools and techniques can be used in strategic analysis, including SWOT analysis, PESTEL analysis, and Porter's Five Forces model.

SWOT analysis involves examining an organization's strengths, weaknesses, opportunities, and threats. This can help identify internal and external factors that may impact the organization's performance.

PESTEL analysis involves examining the political, economic, social, technological, environmental, and legal factors that may impact an organization. This can help identify external forces that may affect the organization's operations and performance.

Porter's Five Forces model involves analyzing the intensity of competition within an industry and identifying the key drivers of competition. This can help an organization understand its competitive position and identify potential growth opportunities.

In addition to these tools and techniques, it is important to consider the organization's mission, vision, and values when conducting a strategic analysis. This can help ensure that the organization's strategic direction aligns with its core values and long-term goals.

Overall, strategic analysis is a critical step in the business improvement process as it helps organizations understand their current situation, identify growth opportunities, and develop a plan for achieving long-term success.

Strategic Objectives

Strategic objectives are long-term goals that an organization sets for itself to achieve its mission and vision. They are the specific targets that the organization aims to achieve to move closer to its overall goals and to create value for its stakeholders.

In business improvement, strategic objectives play a crucial role in helping organizations align their resources and efforts toward achieving their desired outcomes. They provide a clear direction for the organization and help to focus the efforts of employees and other stakeholders toward achieving the desired results.

There are several key factors to consider when developing strategic objectives for business improvement. These include:

1. Alignment with the organization's mission and vision: The strategic objectives should be aligned with the organization's overall mission and vision, and should support the achievement of these goals.

2. Measurable: The objectives should be quantifiable, so that progress can be tracked and evaluated.

3. Achievable: The objectives should be realistic and achievable, given the organization's resources and capabilities.

4. Relevant: The objectives should be relevant to the organization and its stakeholders, and should address the needs and priorities of these groups.

5. Time-bound: The objectives should have a specific timeline for achievement, to provide a sense of urgency and to ensure that progress is being made toward their achievement.

In summary, strategic objectives are an important tool for business improvement, as they provide a clear direction and focus for the organization and help to align the efforts of all stakeholders toward the achievement of the desired outcomes. By setting clear, measurable, achievable, relevant, and time-bound objectives, organizations can improve their performance and create value for their stakeholders.

Strategic implementation

Strategic implementation is the process of taking a business improvement plan and putting it into action. It involves executing the necessary steps to achieve the goals and objectives that have been outlined in the plan. This process is critical for businesses to achieve success and stay competitive in today's marketplace.

Effective strategic implementation requires careful planning and coordination. It involves setting clear goals and objectives, identifying the resources needed to achieve them, and establishing a timeline for completion. It also involves identifying any potential roadblocks or challenges that may arise and developing contingency plans to overcome them.

One key aspect of strategic implementation is the involvement of all relevant stakeholders. This includes employees, customers, suppliers, and other partners who may be impacted by the changes being made. Ensuring that all stakeholders are on board and understand the goals and objectives of the business improvement plan is crucial for its success.

To effectively implement a business improvement plan, it is important to have strong leadership and communication. This includes regular updates on progress, as well as clear and open communication channels to address any concerns or issues that may arise. It is also important to have a system in place to track and measure progress so that any necessary adjustments can be made along the way.

Overall, strategic implementation is a critical part of business improvement. By carefully planning and executing the necessary steps, businesses can achieve their goals and stay competitive in today's marketplace.

CHAPTER FOUR

PROCESS IMPROVEMENT

Process improvement is the systematic identification and implementation of changes to business processes to improve efficiency, effectiveness, and agility. It is a systematic approach to identifying and fixing problems within a business process, intending to increase the overall efficiency and effectiveness of the process.

There are several approaches to process improvement, including Lean, Six Sigma, and the Business Process Management (BPM) method. Each approach has its own set of tools and techniques for identifying and addressing process issues, but all share the same goal of improving the efficiency and effectiveness of business processes.

One key aspect of process improvement is identifying bottlenecks or inefficiencies in the process. These are points in the process where there is a significant delay or reduction in productivity. By identifying and addressing these bottlenecks, organizations can significantly improve the overall efficiency of their processes.

Another important aspect of process improvement is the use of data and metrics to track and analyze the performance of business processes. By collecting data on process performance and analyzing it, organizations can identify trends and patterns that can help them identify areas for improvement.

The process improvement process typically involves a series of steps, including:

Identify the process to be improved: This involves identifying the specific business process that is causing problems or inefficiencies.

Define the current process: This involves creating a detailed map or flowchart of the current process, including all of the steps, inputs, outputs, and stakeholders involved.

Identify problems and opportunities: This involves identifying areas of the process that are causing problems or inefficiencies, as well as areas where improvements could be made.

Develop improvement options: This involves coming up with a range of potential solutions to the identified problems or opportunities.

Select the best improvement option: This involves evaluating the different improvement options and selecting the one that will have the greatest impact on the process.

Implement the improvement: This involves implementing the selected improvement option and monitoring its impact on the process.

Evaluate the results: This involves measuring the impact of the improvement and determining whether it has achieved the desired outcomes.

Process improvement is an ongoing process, as organizations must continuously seek out opportunities to improve their processes to stay competitive. By adopting a systematic approach to process improvement, organizations can improve the efficiency and effectiveness of their business processes, leading to increased productivity and profitability.

Six Sigma is a business improvement methodology that aims to eliminate defects and reduce variability in processes, products, and services. It was developed by

Motorola in the 1980s and has since been widely adopted by companies around the world as a way to improve efficiency, reduce costs, and increase customer satisfaction.

Six Sigma utilizes data-driven decision-making and problem-solving techniques to identify and eliminate defects and variability in processes. It involves a series of steps known as the DMAIC process: **Define, Measure, Analyze, Improve, and Control**.

The Define phase involves identifying the problem or opportunity that needs to be addressed, as well as defining the goals and objectives of the project. The Measure phase involves collecting data and identifying the root causes of the problem. In the Analyze phase, the data is analyzed to identify patterns and trends that can help explain the problem.

The Improve phase involves developing and implementing solutions to address the root causes of the problem, and the Control phase involves establishing processes and controls to ensure that the improvements are sustained over the long term.

One key aspect of Six Sigma is the use of statistical tools and techniques to analyze data and identify problems. This includes the use of control charts, histograms, and other statistical tools to visualize data and identify patterns and trends.

Another key aspect of Six Sigma is the focus on continuous improvement. Rather than simply solving a single problem, Six Sigma aims to create a culture of continuous improvement in which problems are identified and addressed as they arise, rather than waiting for them to become major issues.

In summary, Six Sigma is a business improvement methodology that uses data-driven decision-making and problem-solving techniques to eliminate defects and reduce variability in processes, products, and services. By following the DMAIC process and utilizing statistical tools and techniques, companies can improve efficiency, reduce costs, and increase customer satisfaction.

Value Stream Mapping

Value stream mapping is a process used in business improvement to analyze and design the flow of materials and information required to bring a product or service to a customer. It is a visual representation of all the steps, both value-added and non-value-added, that are involved in creating and delivering a product or service.

The goal of value stream mapping is to identify and eliminate waste, reduce lead time, and improve the overall efficiency of the process. It is a key tool in lean manufacturing and lean management, which are approaches to streamlining business processes and eliminating waste to increase efficiency and profitability.

To create a value stream map, a team begins by identifying the product or service being delivered and the customer who will receive it. Next, the team maps out the current state of the process, including all the steps involved in creating and delivering the product or service. This includes both value-added activities, which directly contribute to the product or service, and non-value-added activities, which do not add value but are necessary for some other reason.

Once the current state of the process has been mapped out, the team can then identify areas of waste and inefficiency. These may include unnecessary steps, long lead times, bottlenecks, or delays caused by inadequate resources or equipment. The team can then work to eliminate these waste areas and streamline the process by redesigning or reorganizing the flow of materials and information.

Finally, the team can create a future state value stream map, which shows how the process will look once the improvements have been made. This allows the team to visualize the improvements and track progress as they work towards their goals.

Value stream mapping is an effective tool for identifying and eliminating waste, reducing lead times, and improving the overall efficiency of a process. By following this process, businesses can increase profitability and provide a better product or service to their customers.

Lean Processes

Lean processes, also known as lean manufacturing is a business improvement approach that aims to maximize customer value while minimizing waste. The goal of lean processes is to create a smooth and efficient flow of work, eliminate waste, and continuously improve processes.

The core principles of lean processes include identifying and eliminating waste, creating flow, and continuously improving processes. Waste, in this context, refers to any activity that does not add value to the customer. Examples of waste include overproduction, unnecessary movement, defects, excess inventory, and unnecessary processing. By identifying and eliminating waste, businesses can streamline their processes and increase efficiency.

Creating flow refers to the smooth and efficient flow of work through the value stream. This includes identifying bottlenecks and addressing them to ensure that work moves smoothly through the process. Continuous improvement, also known as kaizen, is an integral part of lean processes. It involves constantly looking for ways to improve processes and eliminate waste, to reach a state of perfection in which there is no waste.

Lean processes can be applied to any type of business, including manufacturing, service, and healthcare. Some common tools and techniques used in lean processes include value stream mapping, 5S, Kanban, and visual management. These tools help businesses identify and eliminate waste, create flow, and continuously improve processes.

Implementing lean processes can lead to several benefits, including increased efficiency, reduced costs, improved quality, and increased customer satisfaction. However, successfully implementing lean processes requires a culture of continuous improvement and the active participation of all employees. It also requires a willingness to change established processes and the adoption of new tools and techniques.

In conclusion, lean processes are a powerful business improvement approach that can help businesses maximize customer value and minimize waste. By identifying and eliminating waste, creating flow, and continuously improving processes, businesses can increase efficiency, reduce costs, and improve quality.

CHAPTER FIVE

QUALITY IMPROVEMENT

Quality improvement refers to the ongoing process of identifying and addressing issues to improve the overall effectiveness and efficiency of a business. This can be achieved through a variety of methods, including process improvement, Six Sigma, Lean, and other problem-solving techniques.

Total Quality Management (TQM): Total Quality Management is a holistic approach to quality that involves all members of an organization in a continuous effort to improve processes, products, and services. TQM aims to create a culture of quality within an organization, where all employees are committed to meeting and exceeding customer expectations. TQM includes a range of tools and techniques, such as process mapping, root cause analysis, and customer feedback, to identify and address issues to improve overall performance.

Quality Assurance: Quality assurance is the process of verifying that a product or service meets specified standards of quality. This involves designing and implementing processes and procedures to ensure that products and services are consistently delivered to the required standard. Quality assurance can be achieved through testing, inspections, and other means of evaluating product or service quality.

Quality Control: Quality control is the process of ensuring that a product or service meets specified standards of quality. This involves inspecting and testing products or services to ensure that they meet the required specifications. Quality control can be carried out at various stages of the production process, including during design, manufacturing, and distribution.

Overall, implementing quality improvement, TQM, quality assurance, and quality control initiatives can help a business to improve its operations, increase customer satisfaction, and drive growth and success. By continuously monitoring and addressing issues, businesses can ensure that they are delivering high-quality products and services, and position themselves for long-term success

Human Resources Management: Human resources management (HRM) is the strategic and coherent approach to the management of an organization's most valued assets - the people working there who individually and collectively contribute to the achievement of the objectives of the business. The scope of HRM is broad and includes aspects such as recruitment, selection, training and development, performance management, employee relations, and compensation and benefits.

Effective HRM is crucial for the success of any business, as it plays a key role in attracting, retaining, and developing talent within the organization. By providing a positive work environment and opportunities for growth and development, HRM helps to increase employee engagement, productivity, and overall business performance.

Employee Engagement: Employee engagement refers to the extent to which employees are involved in, committed to, and motivated by their work. Engaged employees are more likely to go above and beyond in their job duties, have a positive attitude toward their work, and be less likely to leave the organization.

There are various ways to increase employee engagement, including providing opportunities for professional development, recognizing and rewarding employees for their contributions, promoting a positive work culture, and involving employees in decision-making processes. By fostering employee engagement, organizations can improve employee retention, productivity, and customer satisfaction.

Training and Development: Training and development refer to the activities and programs that are designed to help employees acquire new skills and knowledge, improve their performance, and advance their careers. Training can be provided in various forms, including on-the-job training, formal classroom instruction, and online learning.

Effective training and development programs can help organizations to improve employee skills and knowledge, increase productivity, and reduce turnover. Businesses need to invest in ongoing training and development for their employees to stay competitive and meet the changing needs of the business.

Performance Management: Performance management is the process of setting clear, measurable goals for employees and regularly reviewing and providing feedback on their progress toward meeting those goals. It involves establishing clear expectations for performance and providing regular feedback on how well employees are meeting those expectations.

Effective performance management helps to improve employee performance, increase productivity, and drive business results. It also provides an opportunity for employees to discuss their goals, career aspirations, and areas for improvement with their managers. By regularly reviewing and tracking performance, organizations can identify areas for improvement and provide support and resources to help employees achieve their full potential.

Overall, HRM, employee engagement, training and development, and performance management are all important factors in business improvement. By effectively managing and developing their workforce, organizations can increase productivity, improve employee retention, and drive overall business success.

Technology, automation, data analysis, and cloud computing can all play a significant role in improving business operations and outcomes. Here's a brief overview of each of these technologies and how they can be used to benefit businesses:

1. **Technology:** The use of technology can greatly improve the efficiency, accuracy, and speed of various business processes. For example, companies can use technology to automate tasks such as invoicing, payroll, and customer service, freeing

up time and resources for more strategic endeavors.

2. **Automation:** Automation involves the use of technology to perform tasks without the need for human intervention. This can be especially useful for businesses that have repetitive or time-consuming processes, such as data entry or product assembly. Automation can increase efficiency and accuracy, while also reducing the risk of human error.

3. **Data analysis:** The vast amount of data generated by businesses today can be overwhelming and difficult to make sense of. Data analysis tools allow businesses to extract valuable

insights and trends from their data, which can inform decision-making and drive business growth.

4. **Cloud computing:** Cloud computing refers to the delivery of computing services, such as storage, processing, networking, and more, over the Internet. By moving these resources to the cloud, businesses can save on infrastructure and maintenance costs, while also enjoying greater flexibility and scalability.

In summary, the use of technology, automation, data analysis, and cloud computing can greatly improve the efficiency and effectiveness of business operations. By leveraging these technologies, businesses can increase productivity, drive growth, and stay ahead of the competition.

CONCLUSION

It is important to continually strive for improvement in any business. This can involve analyzing and identifying areas for improvement, setting goals and implementing strategies to achieve those goals, and regularly reviewing and adjusting your approach to ensure ongoing progress. Some specific areas where businesses may look for improvement include increasing efficiency, reducing costs, enhancing customer satisfaction, expanding market reach, and increasing profitability.

To achieve these improvements, businesses may consider implementing process improvements, adopting new technologies, training and developing employees, and seeking input and feedback from customers and stakeholders. Ultimately, the key to business improvement is to continuously assess and adapt your operations to ensure that you are meeting the needs of your customers and stakeholders and achieving your business goals

www.ingramcontent.com/pod-product-compliance
Lightning Source LLC
LaVergne TN
LVHW050339160826
845677LV00014B/3691
9798370430473